John C

By Lynn Peppas

Crabtree Publishing Company
www.crabtreebooks.com

Crabtree Publishing Company

www.crabtreebooks.com

Dedicated by Katherine Berti
To hotshot hubby Matty from diva wifey Kitty.
For the Hulkamaniac in your heart and Undertaker in your soul.

Author: Lynn Peppas
Publishing plan research and development:
  Sean Charlebois, Reagan Miller
  Crabtree Publishing Company
Coordinating editor: Paul Humphrey
Editorial director: Kathy Middleton
Editors: Crystal Sikkens, Gianna Williams
Photo researcher: Gianna Williams
Proofreader: Wendy Scavuzzo
Designer: sprout.uk.com
Series design: Ken Wright
Production coordinator and
  prepress technician: Ken Wright
Print coordinator: Katherine Berti

Produced for the Crabtree Publishing Company
by Discovery Books

Photographs:
Alamy: @Allstar Picture Library: pages 4, 10, 25;
  @ZUMA Press, Inc: pages 5, 17 bottom;
  @ZUMA Wire Service: page 7; @PixelPro: page
  13; @AF Archive: pages 22, 24; @Moviestore
  Collection Ltd: page 26
AP Images: @Associated Press: page 18; @Jeff
  Daly/Picture Group: page 21
Corbis: @David Yellen: page 16; @Ray Lego/ Corbis
  Outline: page 9
Getty: @FilmMagic: page 14; @WireImage: page 12
©wenn.com/KEYSTONE Press: cover
Shutterstock: @Juli Hansen: page 23; @Helga Esteb:
  page 28
Wikimedia: Staff Sgt. James Selesnick: page 6; Felipe
  Bascunan: page 17 top; Simononly: page 27; Spc
  Shantelle J. Campbell, 41BCT PAO: page 20;
  Shamsuddin Muhammad: page 1

This book is not an official WWE publication.
WWE is not associated, affiliated, or endorsing
the contents of this book.

Library and Archives Canada Cataloguing in Publication

Peppas, Lynn
       John Cena / Lynn Peppas.

(Superstars!)
Includes index.
Issued also in electronic format.
ISBN 978-0-7787-8052-6 (bound).--ISBN 978-0-7787-8057-1 (pbk.)

       1. Cena, John--Juvenile literature. 2. Wrestlers--United
States--Biography--Juvenile literature. 3. Motion picture actors
and actresses--United States--Biography--Juvenile literature.
I. Title. II. Series: Superstars! (St. Catharines, Ont.)

GV1196.C46P46 2012   j796.812092   C2012-906754-7

Library of Congress Cataloging-in-Publication Data

Peppas, Lynn.
     John Cena / by Lynn Peppas.
         p. cm. -- (Superstars!)
     Includes index.
     ISBN 978-0-7787-8052-6 (reinforced library binding) -- ISBN
   978-0-7787-8057-1 (pbk.) -- ISBN 978-1-4271-9071-0 (electronic (pdf))
   -- ISBN 978-1-4271-9125-0 (electronic (html))
     1. Cena, John--Juvenile literature. 2. Wrestlers--United States--
Biography--Juvenile literature. I. Title.

  GV1196.C46P47 2012
  796.812092--dc23
  [B]
                                                       2012040231

Crabtree Publishing Company

www.crabtreebooks.com   1-800-387-7650

Printed in the U.S.A./112012/FA20121012

Published in Canada
Crabtree Publishing
616 Welland Ave.
St. Catharines, ON
L2M 5V6

Published in the United States
Crabtree Publishing
PMB 59051
350 Fifth Avenue, 59th Floor
New York, New York 10118

Published in the United Kingdom
Crabtree Publishing
Maritime House
Basin Road North, Hove
BN41 1WR

Published in Australia
Crabtree Publishing
386 Mt. Alexander Rd.
Ascot Vale (Melbourne)
VIC 3032

CONTENTS

Words that are defined in the glossary are in
bold type the first time they appear in the text.

Wrestling with Superstardom

John Cena has wrestled his way to the top of superstardom. The 35-year-old sports entertainer is the "face" of WWE (World Wrestling Entertainment). When a wrestler is a face, it means they play a character that is a good guy or a hero. In his 10-plus years at WWE, Cena's "face" value has gained him 12 WWE titles. He shows no sign of retiring in the near future. His clean-cut good looks, chiseled jawline, and muscular **physique** suit his "good guy" image.

Cena Buff

It is a full-time job to stay in shape like John Cena. The superstar wrestler works at keeping his body the lean, muscular machine that it is by working out at least five days a week. It is hard to believe that in his first year at high school he weighed 120 lbs (54 kg). He started weight training when he was 12 years old. By the end of high school, Cena had doubled his weight to more than 240 lbs (109 kg).

John Cena's signature hip-hop fashion sense in the ring almost always includes knee-length jean shorts.

Sporting his merchandise with popular slogans "U Can't See Me" and "Rise Above Hate," John Cena is interviewed before his "once in a lifetime match" with The Rock for Wrestlemania 28.

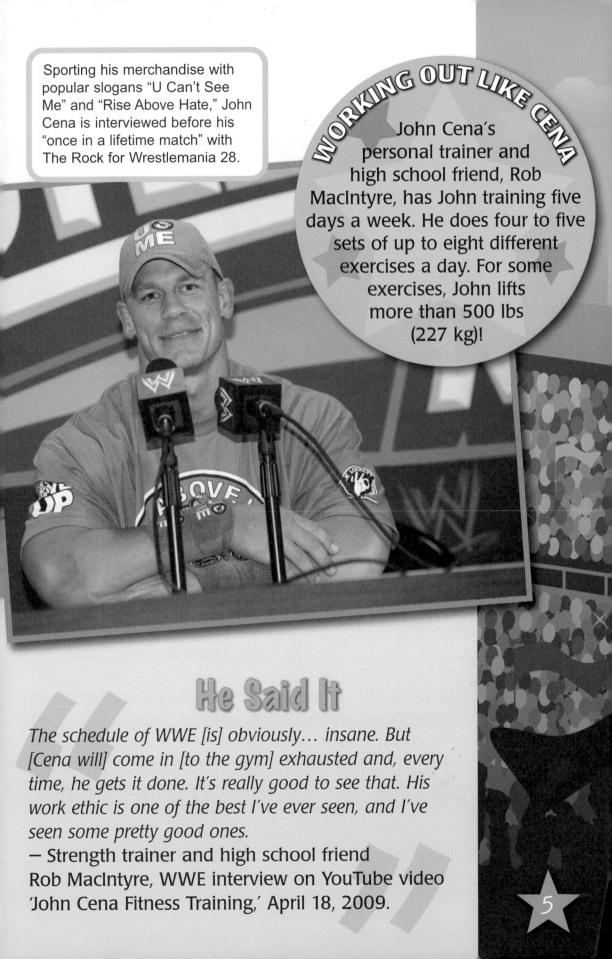

WORKING OUT LIKE CENA

John Cena's personal trainer and high school friend, Rob MacIntyre, has John training five days a week. He does four to five sets of up to eight different exercises a day. For some exercises, John lifts more than 500 lbs (227 kg)!

He Said It

The schedule of WWE [is] obviously... insane. But [Cena will] come in [to the gym] exhausted and, every time, he gets it done. It's really good to see that. His work ethic is one of the best I've ever seen, and I've seen some pretty good ones.

– Strength trainer and high school friend Rob MacIntyre, WWE interview on YouTube video 'John Cena Fitness Training,' April 18, 2009.

Ringside Manners

Part of Cena's charm is his intensity and confidence in the ring. For most professional wrestling entertainers, these traits come across as **arrogant**—but not with Cena. He has a humble, straightforward manner. He knows that on a bad day he can be beaten and he handles defeat with class. Cena's famous **slogan**, "Hustle, Loyalty, and Respect," says it all. He is one of WWE's most hard-working, loyal, and respectful sport entertainers. He practices it in the ring and outside, too. "Mentally if you want it bad enough you can go beyond what your body is capable of. I do what I do. I'm not the most technical guy out there. But I will fight. And I will get my [butt] kicked. And I'll stand up and say, 'Is that all you got?'"

Tall, strong, and handsome, Cena is the perfect face for both wrestling and movies.

OUTSIDE OF THE RING

Cena's good looks and musical talents have translated into a film and music career that goes beyond his work in the ring. With a score of movies and a **debut** rap album, *You Can't See Me*, Cena has proved that he has brains as well as **brawn**.

A Love/Hate Relationship with Fans

There really is no middle ground when it comes to how WWE fans feel about John Cena. They either love him or hate him. A large number of Cena's fans are young people and women. Most like his clean-cut looks and his good-guy hero image. Many look up to him as a role model. Most older WWE fans don't like Cena's squeaky clean, "goody-two-shoes" image, or the fact that he has lasted longer in WWE than many other wrestlers. Cena says he doesn't really care whether people love him or hate him. He simply wants to entertain people.

WINNING CHARM

From 2006-2010 Cena enjoyed a five-year run of being named "Most **Charismatic**" wrestler by the *Wrestling Observer Newsletter*.

Cena is about to do a Diving Leg Drop Bulldog on an **opponent**.

He Said It

I don't care about whether my character is positive or negative. What I want is electricity in the air, which gives me something to work with. It doesn't matter if they are cheering me or booing.
—Online interview, Tellychakkar.com, February 15, 2006

Growing Pains

John Cena has many natural abilities. He's a talented actor, athlete, and musician. Cena's talents are perfect for his wrestling **persona** and movie roles. He has all the right characteristics to make a superstar career.

The climb to the top of superstardom is never easy. Cena has put a lot of hard work into his craft. He is respected as one of the hardest working performers in the sports entertainment business.

Cena's Early Years

John Felix Anthony Cena was born on April 23, 1977, in West Newbury, Massachusetts. West Newbury is a small town with a population of less than 5,000 people. He is the second-oldest son in a family of five boys. At the age of 12, Cena says he was picked on by others because he "didn't fit in with everybody." He decided to take up weightlifting for self-defense.

He Said It

The only time my brothers and I could beat up on each other and get away with it was when we were watching wrestling with my dad!
—Interview in *People* magazine, October 23, 2006

A Family Trade

Wrestling runs in Cena's family. John's father worked as an announcer under the name of Johnny Fabulous for Chaotic Wrestling in Massachusetts. "My old man was a pretty good guy. He didn't realize what he was doing at the time but he was self-employed, self-made and raised five… horrible sons… But at a young age… he showed us that there is no **substitute** for hard work to succeed and get the things you want in life."

John Cena poses in front of the Hard Nock's Gym in Amesbury, Massachusetts.

He Said It

I'm always using John as an example, that here's what you are today and here's what you can be. Kids can look at him and say, 'Wow, you mean he came from high school around here?'… So he's been a role model for a lot of the kids around here. And a good role model.
–Hard Nock's Gym owner, Dave Nock, video 'John Cena Fitness Training,' April 18, 2009.

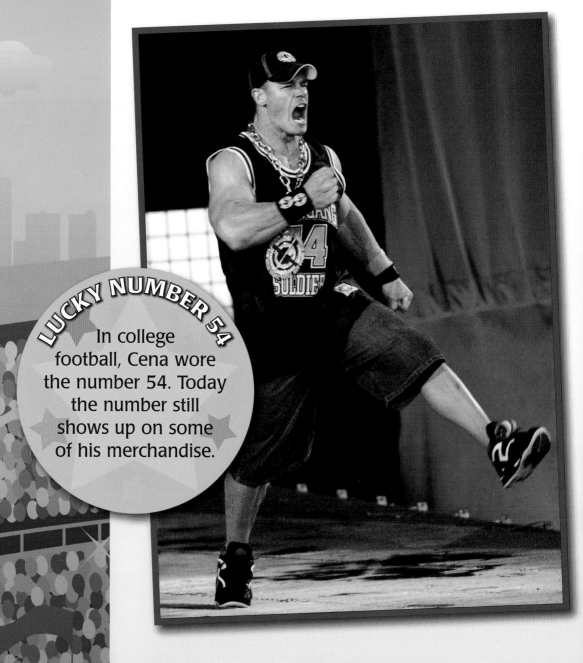

LUCKY NUMBER 54

In college football, Cena wore the number 54. Today the number still shows up on some of his merchandise.

He Said It

If there was ever a definition of working class, it's me. [Early in high school] I learned that you really just have to work for everything you have. And I learned to work hard. Put your helmet on, go to practice until you can't practice anymore, and then go some more.
—In WWE interview posted on YouTube, February 10, 2012, as "John Cena Workout"

10

College and Ultimate University Years

During his high school and college years, Cena was best known for his football-playing abilities as an **offensive lineman**. After graduation, he continued to bodybuild while working odd jobs at different gyms. He also worked as a limousine driver. In January 2000, at the age of 22, he decided to study wrestling at Ultimate University in California. Ultimate University is a professional wrestling school run by the sports entertainment company Ultimate Pro Wrestling. Cena fought in the ring for Ultimate Pro Wrestling and won the UPW Heavyweight Championship in April 2000.

A DEGREE OF SKILL
John Cena graduated from Springfield College in 1998 with a degree in Exercise Physiology, which is the study of how exercise affects people.

The Prototype

In 2001, the WWE or World Wrestling Entertainment (then called the WWF or World Wrestling Federation) offered Cena a developmental contract. This meant that he was part of the WWE, but he first needed to gain experience wrestling in a smaller circuit. To receive his training, Cena was sent to Ohio Valley Wrestling (OVW), which was the WWE's developmental territory in Louisville, Kentucky. During his time there, Cena wrestled under the character name The Prototype. Prototype means the first of something. He won the OVW Heavyweight Championship and held it for three months.

Cena's TV Debut

In 2002, Cena was promoted to WWE's main **roster**. Then on June 27, he got his television debut on WWE's show *SmackDown*. Inspired by a speech given by WWE's **Chairman** and **CEO**, Vince McMahon, he accepted an open challenge to fight pro wrestler Kurt Angle. He was determined to show his "ruthless aggression," as prompted by McMahon, and gain a place at the top as one of the legends. During the match, Cena gave a good fight. But, in the end, Angle took the win. Cena didn't win the match, but he did win over the crowd and became one of the fan favorites.

Kurt Angle is the only professional wrestler who has ever won an Olympic gold medal in wrestling.

The Doctor Is In

In the beginning of his career in the WWE, Cena's **gimmick** was very different from the one he has today. During the 2002 Halloween episode of *SmackDown*, he established his major heel character. A heel is known by fans as a bad guy. Dressed as the rapper Vanilla Ice, he debuted his rap routine and became known as the "Doctor of Thuganomics."

Cena's edgy and ruthless "Doctor of Thuganomics" character came into the ring rapping and wearing an NBA (National Basketball Association) Cleveland Cavaliers jersey, and a heavy lock chain. Cena was often compared to actor Mark Wahlberg's rapper **alter ego** called Marky Mark. Some even went so far as to call Cena the "Marky Mark of wrestling."

Cena's style, which includes baggy and belted knee-length jean shorts or camouflage-pattern shorts, came after his debut as the Doctor of Thuganomics. You can also see him in baseball caps and T-shirts with his own logos such as "Rise Above Hate."

John Cena is shown wearing his Cleveland Cavaliers baseball cap.

13

John Cena and Tha Trademarc cash in on their debut album, *You Can't See Me*, released in May 2005.

The Rap on John Cena

Cena built his wrestling career around his rapper gimmick, but how much of a gimmick was it really? The talented **MC** performed freestyle raps such as "Basic Thuganomics," released on WWE **compilation** album *WWE Originals* in 2004 and "Untouchables," released on *ThemeAddict: WWE The Music*, Vol. 6 in 2007. Cena co-wrote "Untouchables" and performed it with his cousin, Marc Predka, who goes by the hip-hop name of "Tha Trademarc."

A Musical Hit

Cena and Tha Trademarc worked on Cena's debut album called *You Can't See Me*, (WWE, 2005). The album sold more than 140,000 copies in the first week. It rose to number 15 on Billboard's 200 chart. Other hip-hop artists such as Bumpy Knuckles and Esoteric were featured on some of the album tracks, too. The album includes the song "The Time Is Now," which became Cena's WWE entrance song.

Cena grew up listening to hip-hop and is a huge fan of the music. Five of his favorite hip-hop albums of all time are Jay-Z's *Black Album*, Kanye West's *The College Dropout*, The Beastie Boys' *Licensed to Ill*, Snoop Dogg's *Doggystyle*, and N.W.A.'s *Straight Outta Compton*.

He Said It

*(Music) was the **facet** that opened the door for me. The rap idea came along totally by accident. Somebody at WWE heard me rapping and said, 'Hey, why don't we get this on television?' That's what got me on the map. It was the right time, just as hip-hop was at its peak.*
—In a *Sky Sports* magazine interview with Jon Hotten, March 2010

WWE Championships and Belts

The WWE awards its winning wrestlers with different championship titles. WWE titles for male heavyweight wrestlers include the United States Championship, the World Heavyweight Championship, the Intercontinental Championship, the WWE Tag Team Championship, and the WWE Championship. The WWE Championship is considered to be the highest-ranking championship title in the WWE. Each title awards a different championship belt. Some popular wrestlers, such as John Cena, The Rock, and The Miz, have designed their own WWE Championship belts.

John Cena's personalized WWE Championship belt has a center plate that spins.

Since his first WWE Championship win on April 3, 2005, Cena has won ten WWE Championships and three United States Championships. He also won the World Heavyweight Championship two times, in November 2008 and in April 2009. His Tag Team Championships, won with the help of WWE wrestlers David Otunga and The Miz, total two.

THE BIG SHOW

Cena won his first-ever United States Championship on March 14, 2004, when he defeated the wrestler, Big Show, at Wrestlemania XX.

The Attitude Adjustment

There are certain moves that every pro wrestler is known for that get their fans cheering when they unleash them in the ring. These signature moves serve as an individual trademark for that wrestler. Cena's main signature move is known as the Attitude Adjustment. It was once called The FU, but Cena decided to change the name when he realized his audience was starting to include more children. Most wrestlers are down for the count after they have had an Attitude Adjustment!

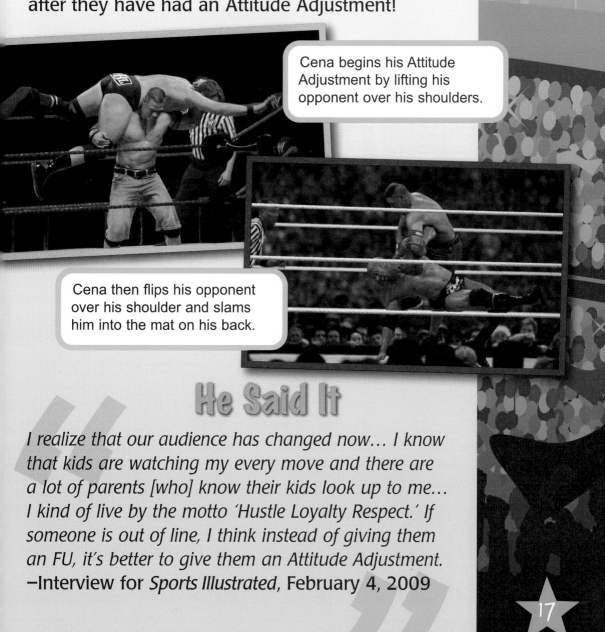

Cena begins his Attitude Adjustment by lifting his opponent over his shoulders.

Cena then flips his opponent over his shoulder and slams him into the mat on his back.

He Said It

I realize that our audience has changed now… I know that kids are watching my every move and there are a lot of parents [who] know their kids look up to me… I kind of live by the motto 'Hustle Loyalty Respect.' If someone is out of line, I think instead of giving them an FU, it's better to give them an Attitude Adjustment.
—Interview for *Sports Illustrated*, February 4, 2009

Hustle, Loyalty, and Respect

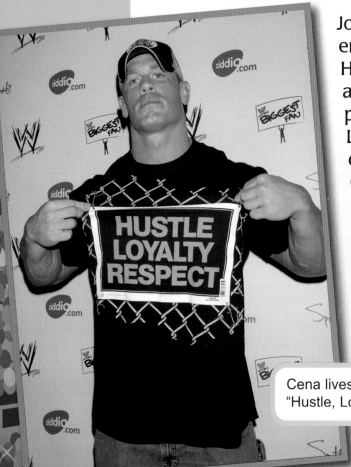

John Cena is all about entertaining the WWE fans. He is devoted to his sport and really knows how to pour on the "Hustle, Loyalty, and Respect." The combination has rewarded Cena with a long and popular career in WWE. It isn't always an easy lifestyle. Cena has had to work hard for his fame and fortune.

Cena lives his life by his motto "Hustle, Loyalty, and Respect."

He Said It

Professional wrestling isn't like other pro sports where you might get a four-day home stand. I travel over 300 days a year. We do a different city every night. We go all over. It's a day-by-day thing. You have to really learn to hustle.
—Interview posted in 2004 on http://mrjoewalkerpresents.blogspot.ca/2011/03/

Fighting for Celebrity Status

Cena has enjoyed his share of celebrity gimmicks that have helped his status climb as a superstar wrestler. On New Year's Day in 2007, Cena fought dancer and rapper Kevin Federline who was then married to superstar singer Britney Spears. At the time, Federline was promoting his own album *Playing with Fire*. Federline was joined by WWE wrestler Johnny Nitro and together they defeated Cena in the non-title match. Later, after the fight, Cena earned back some respect when he performed the Attitude Adjustment finishing move on Federline—not once, but twice!

Hazards of Professional Wrestling

Even though the storylines of WWE are **scripted**, accidents can happen and many wrestlers have ended up with injuries. Many of the wrestling moves performed in this sport involve lifting and throwing other wrestlers that weigh close to, or more than, 300 lbs (136 kg). Cena has had his share of injuries, including one in which he tore his pectoral major muscle in his upper chest. It happened during a fight in October 2007 with WWE wrestler, Mr. Kennedy. Cena had to have surgery and it took months afterward for him to **recuperate**.

INJURIES AND SURGERY

Cena underwent surgery in 2008 on his neck following an injury during a match against pro wrestler Batista, and again in September 2012 for his elbow injury, caused by years of wear and tear in the ring.

Cena's Softer Side

Cena might play the tough guy in WWE's wrestling ring, but behind the scenes he has a softer side. Cena has taken part in WWE's Tribute to the Troops. This involves WWE wrestlers traveling to overseas countries to visit different American military bases, camps, and hospitals. Cena has traveled to Iraq four times and Afghanistan once.

Cena is also a champion when it comes to making sick kids' wishes come true at the Make-A-Wish Foundation. Make-A-Wish Foundation is a non-profit organization that grants wishes to children with life-threatening illnesses. In 2012, Cena held the record for the number of wishes granted by one person.

Cena supports U.S. troops by entertaining them while they are stationed in Iraq.

He Said It

There's nothing greater than seeing a Make-A-Wish child... get so excited, so happy and pretty much be welcomed into the escape that is the WWE... That's pretty much what it's all about for me.
—Interview on *Good Morning Arizona*, January 23, 2012.

Wedding Bells and Break-up

John Cena asked his high school sweetheart, Elizabeth (called Liz by her friends) Huberdeau, to marry him in 2007. Liz grew up in the same small town as Cena did, in West Newbury, Massachusetts. They have known each other for most of their lives. Liz went to the same high school and college as John. The two lovebirds tied the knot in Boston, Massachusetts, on July 11, 2009. However Cena and Liz's marriage lasted less than three years. The couple divorced in May 2012.

THE ROMANTIC SIDE OF CENA

In interviews, Cena has admitted to being kind of a "shy guy" when it comes to the ladies. He admitted to not being able to talk confidently around women he has just met.

Cena and his wife Liz visit the Daytona International Speedway only three months before their break-up.

Cena on the Big Screen

In 2003, the WWE set up a movie production studio and since then has turned its best-known wrestlers into actors. One of the most famous wrestler-turned-actors is The Rock—Dwayne Johnson—who left the WWE ring in 2003 to pursue his acting career. John Cena made his acting debut in 2006 in the WWE Studios movie *The Marine*. In it he plays the role of a U.S. Marine named John Triton. Cena's character is a hero who saves a group of Marines from **execution** by terrorists and later rescues his wife. *The Marine* was released in theaters on October 13, 2006. It earned over $7 million in its first week at the box office and over $22 million internationally.

John Cena lit up the silver screen in his debut movie, *The Marine*, released in 2006.

All-round Actor

Twelve Rounds was the next major action film that Cena starred in. In this film, he plays a police detective named Danny Fisher. After he helps put a terrorist criminal behind bars, the criminal escapes and kidnaps Fisher's wife. Fisher must accomplish 12 nearly impossible tasks to save his wife's life. The film brought in over $17 million worldwide.

John Cena acting on the set for his action-packed, blockbuster movie *Twelve Rounds*.

In 2010, Cena starred in the movie *Legendary*. He plays a character named Mike Chetley, a former wrestling champ who now coaches wrestling at high school level. This movie drew a lot more from the emotional side of Cena. When Cena first read the script, he fell in love with the story and knew he had to be a part of it. It did not do as well at the box office as Cena's other films, however, and only brought in just over $120,000 in its first weekend.

THE REUNION

Cena starred in an another action film called *The Reunion* in 2011. Cena played the oldest of three brothers who don't get along. After the death of their father, the brothers must work together to cash in on a large inheritance.

The Fred Movies

Can Cena do comedy? Well, yes he can, and he's proved it in his acting roles in the *Fred* movies. The first *Fred* film was originally made for movie theaters but was sold to the children's TV channel, Nickelodeon, instead. *Fred: The Movie* was first aired on September 18, 2010. In it, Cena plays Fred's "imaginary" father who pops up from time to time to offer advice and support to Fred when he needs it most. On the first night it aired on television, the movie had over seven million viewers.

A **sequel** called *Fred 2: Night of the Living Fred* was released on Nickelodeon channel on October 22, 2011. The sequel drew over five million viewers on its first showing.

FRED 3: CAMP FRED

Cena stepped up once again to play Fred's imaginary father, Mr. Figglehorn, for the third *Fred* movie *Camp Fred* shown on Nickelodeon TV. It was first aired on July 28, 2012 and was watched by over three million viewers.

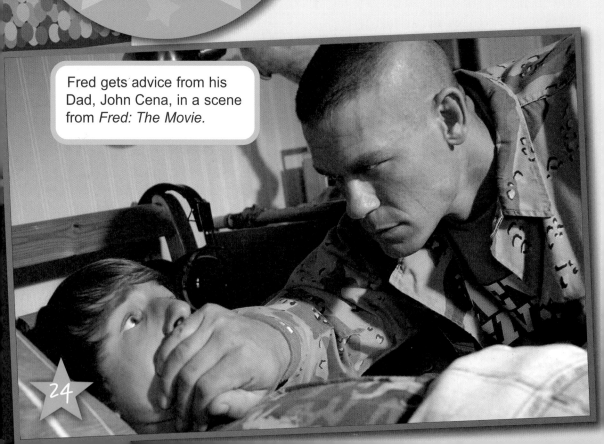

Fred gets advice from his Dad, John Cena, in a scene from *Fred: The Movie.*

In the Limelight

Cena's growing popularity has also landed him numerous television appearances on talk shows such as *Jimmy Kimmel* and *Late Night with Conan O'Brien*. He made a guest appearance as himself in an episode of *Hannah Montana* and got *"Punk'd"* by Ashton Kutcher in 2007. He tried his hand at racecar driving in the TV reality show *Fast Cars and Superstars: The Gillette Young Guns Celebrity Race* in 2007. In it, Cena lost to Broncos quarterback John Elway but placed a respectable third place overall.

Cena co-presented at the Teen Choice Awards in 2005 with wrestling star Hulk Hogan.

He Said It

"Fred was so nice that we had to do it twice. I'm very excited to be back for Fred 2: Night of the Living Fred... I know you either love Fred or you hate Fred, which means I think I belong in this movie because I'm one of those guys. You either love me or you hate me."
—Interview on WWE.com,
October 20, 2011

The Time Is Now

Up Against The Rock...

John Cena's wrestling storyline is ongoing. As the face of WWE, Cena has had to take on some tough opponents during his 10-plus years in the business. Popular fights have taken place between Cena and other WWE wrestlers such as Triple H, C.M. Punk, Chris Jericho, Randy Orton, The Miz, Sheamus, Rey Mysterio, and many, many others.

In 2011, tension began to build with former WWE Heavyweight Champion and superstar actor, Dwayne Johnson, otherwise known as "The Rock." The Rock returned to WWE wrestling after having been retired since 2003. The Rock and Cena taunted each other in separate interviews and WWE episodes of *Raw*. Cena accused The Rock of not being true to his fans at WWE. Critics accused Cena of being jealous of the success of The Rock's acting career in movies.

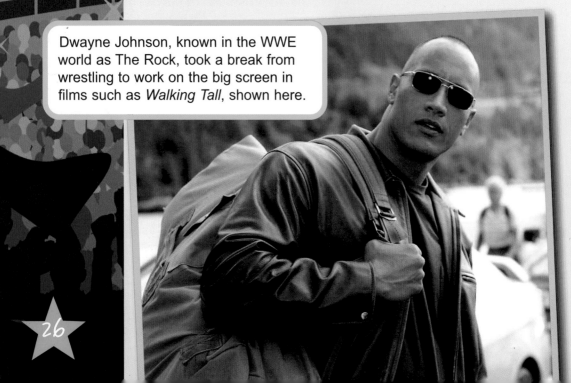

Dwayne Johnson, known in the WWE world as The Rock, took a break from wrestling to work on the big screen in films such as *Walking Tall*, shown here.

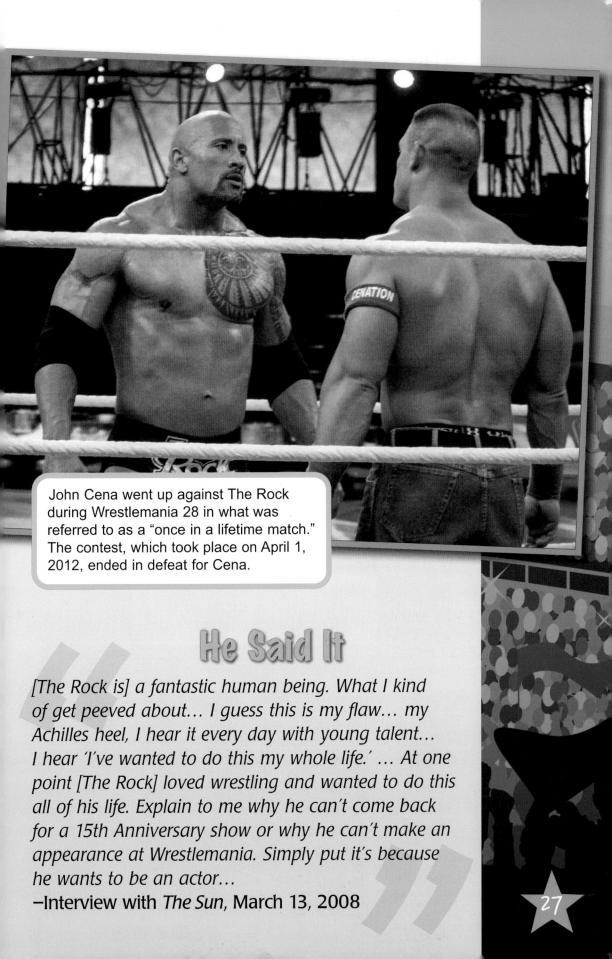

John Cena went up against The Rock during Wrestlemania 28 in what was referred to as a "once in a lifetime match." The contest, which took place on April 1, 2012, ended in defeat for Cena.

He Said It

[The Rock is] a fantastic human being. What I kind of get peeved about... I guess this is my flaw... my Achilles heel, I hear it every day with young talent... I hear 'I've wanted to do this my whole life.' ... At one point [The Rock] loved wrestling and wanted to do this all of his life. Explain to me why he can't come back for a 15th Anniversary show or why he can't make an appearance at Wrestlemania. Simply put it's because he wants to be an actor...

−Interview with *The Sun*, March 13, 2008

Still a Winner

John Cena seems to have had his hand in all aspects of entertaining from his wrestling career to acting roles to rapping. So, what's next for John Cena—a new album, new movie role, or a grueling match with one of his rivals? Only time will tell, but he does plan to continue being someone children can look up to and has his sights on breaking pro wrestler Ric Flair's 16 World Championship record. When you see him next, you can be sure his fans will be there sporting their John Cena merchandise displaying his famous slogans "Rise Above Hate" and "Hustle, Loyalty, and Respect."

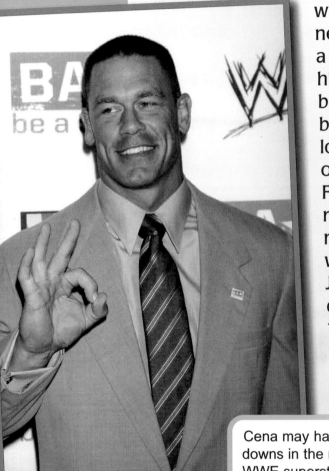

Cena may have his ups and downs in the ring, but life for the WWE superstar is obviously A-OK.

He Said It

"*Even though you may be trained in your craft there is still intense physical punishment... [Professional wrestlers] carry this torch 365 days a year... and go out and risk our lives every time we do it. That's why we have to be trained. Everything hurts. You can be as trained as you want to be, but everything still hurts.*"
—Interview in 2004 on
http://mrjoewalkerpresents.blogspot.ca/2011/03/

Timeline

April 23, 1977: John Felix Anthony Cena is born in West Newbury, Massachusetts.

January 2000: John Cena studies wrestling at the Ultimate University in California.

April 2000: John Cena wins the UPW (Ultimate Pro Wrestling) Heavyweight Championship.

2001: Cena signs a contract with WWF (World Wrestling Federation, later known as WWE). He begins his professional career with OVW (Ohio Valley Wrestling).

February 2002: Cena wins the OVW Heavyweight Championship.

June 27, 2002: Cena makes his WWE debut in a fight with WWE wrestler, Kurt Angle.

January 13, 2004: Cena's hip-hop song, "Basic Thugonomics," is released.

March 14, 2004: Cena wins his first-ever WWE title —the United States Championship.

November 16, 2004: Cena's hip-hop song, "Untouchables," is released.

April 3, 2005: Cena wins the WWE Championship.

May 10, 2005: Cena's debut album, *You Can't See Me*, is released in the United States.

October 13, 2006: Cena stars in *The Marine*.

November 2008: Cena wins the World Heavyweight Championship for the first time.

January 1, 2007: Cena fights Kevin Federline.

October 2007: Cena tears a muscle in his upper chest, needing surgery.

March 27, 2009: *Twelve Rounds* is released in theaters.

July 11, 2009: Cena marries Elizabeth Huberdeau.

October 21, 2011: Cena appears in *The Reunion*.

April 1, 2012: Cena is defeated by The Rock at Wrestlemania 28.

May 2012: Cena and his wife divorce.

Glossary

alter ego A second or opposite side of a person's personality

arrogant The quality of a person acting like they are more important, or better, than others

brawn A strong and muscular body

CEO Stands for Chief Executive Officer. A CEO is the highest ranking person or leader who oversees the management of a company.

chairman The chief officer in charge of a business

charismatic Appealing and interesting to other people

compilation A thing that is built or made up of many different collected pieces or parts

debut The first

execution To kill someone as a form of punishment

facet An aspect or feature of something

gimmick An idea or plan designed to bring attention to something

MC Stands for microphone controller; a hip-hop musical performer

offensive lineman A football player who defends the quarterback

opponent In sports, the player or team who competes against another

persona A character or role performed by a person

physique A person's body

recuperate To get better or stronger

roster A list of people involved in an organization

scripted A series of events that are written and planned for actors to follow

sequel The next part in a series

slogan A short and catchy phrase that advertises something

substitute Thing that takes the place of something else

Find Out More

Books

O'Shei, Tim. *Stars of Pro Wrestling: John Cena*. North Mankato, MN: Capstone Press, 2009.

Shields, Brian. *WWE: John Cena*. St. Louis, MO: Turtleback Books, 2009.

Websites

The WWE's website
www.wwe.com/superstars/

A John Cena fan club website
www.j-cena.com

John Cena's Myspace page
www.myspace.com/
officialjohncenamusicpage/

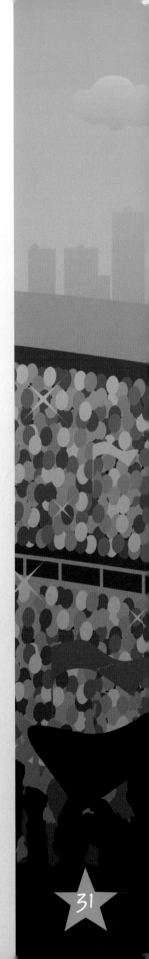

Index

About the Author

Lynn Peppas is the author of over 60 children's non-fiction books and the mother of five children. She has worked in the publishing industry as a freelance author and editor for over a dozen years. When not reading or writing she enjoys cooking, biking, and nature hikes. She lives in the small town with her family and her tortoiseshell cat named Bee-zoo.